I0797115

The Book of Red Flags

Laugh, cry,
or commiserate.
Dating is an
absolute nightmare.

Dating Signs They Aren't It

The Book of Red Flags

JENNY GORELICK

Illustrations by Margalit Cutler

RIZZOLI UNIVERSE

Table of Contents

To all my exes.

If we flirted one time for
five minutes, you're also my ex,
and this is for you.

Introduction

DATING THESE DAYS IS AN ABSOLUTE NIGHTMARE. If you picked up this book, I assume you agree. You're out on the town, you're on the apps, you're trying to meet someone to settle down with or at least take you apple picking for once. And it's not going awesome. It's mostly bad apples.

You're screaming into the void, "WHY AM I STILL SINGLE?!" Or maybe that's what your mom said when she gifted this to you. (Mom, leave her alone! She'll meet someone! Eventually! God willing! Personally, I'm an atheist, but I'm at the point where I'll find God if that means I'll also find a husband.)

Being thirty-three years old and single in New York City isn't easy. If it were, we wouldn't have six seasons of *Sex and the City* AND two movies. So, I couldn't help but wonder, isn't it all worth it? (And since you asked, I'm a Carrie, obviously. I wrote this.)

While my friends are out here getting engaged, I'm going on date after date with guys who check all the boxes—he has a good job, his own apartment, and most of his hair—yet, I'm still left heartbroken when I'm ghosted again. Or worse, we date for over three months, and he drops a bomb like, "I'm not looking for anything serious right now." (I'm sorry, we dated for almost an entire fiscal quarter. Is that not serious to you?)

From May to July, I dated two different guys named Sam. Not at the same time, there are just a lot of guys named Sam. Both of their dating app profiles suggested they were looking for girlfriends. They were both in their mid-thirties, so their prefrontal cortexes were done cooking. Check! They had great jobs—one was a consultant and the other in real estate development. Check! They both lived in nice, clean, one-bedroom apartments, and they took me on dinner dates and paid for the full meal. Oh, and the sex was good. Check, check, check!

After seeing each other consistently for over a month, Consultant Sam freaked out. One second, we're on a dinner and movie date, the next he's breaking up with me! While I'm pants-less! Obviously after a dinner and a movie comes sex. Not a breakup! And he didn't pay for my Uber home. What the fuck!?

Then, after a few weeks of dates with Real Estate Sam, he stopped texting me when we had tentative plans to hang out. I called him out, texting, "I get the message." He replied, "There is no 'message.' I'm just busy." A week later, he sent me a breakup text. What. The. Fuck. I gave you an out, sir. You didn't take it. Then you dumped me A WEEK LATER after I asked, are you dumping me? WHAT THE FUCK?!

NOT BOTH SAMS! How much can a girl take?!

But I shouldn't have been so surprised. I was overlooking some vital Red Flags.

What's a Red Flag, you ask? Oh, honey, it's a big fat red SOS warning sign of danger when it comes to dating. It's the hazard sign for a wet floor. Slip, and you might fall in love with a douchebag. It's a poisonous frog with brightly colored skin. Don't touch! He looks cute, but he might kill you.

If there is anything I've learned in my decade of dating—okay, two decades, almost three if you count my kindergarten boyfriend Jack (call me if you're still single, I'll move back to Ohio, I'll try anything)—it is how to spot a Red Flag.

And I almost always run straight to them and play games like Capture the Flag. I have so many points!! Let's tally them up! Did I win? Do I get a prize? Oh, it's HPV!

In the past year alone, I had drinks with a guy who was wearing sunglasses in every photo in his dating app profile. Ten points. I went on a date with a finance guy who said he was going to pick me up in what I assumed was a car, but then rolled up on a motorcycle. One hundred points. And I dated a stand-up comedian for two years. Ding ding ding! One thousand point bonus!!!!

From my years of boots-on-the-ground research, I can identify the little markers that this person is not MY person so that I can move on to the next.

How many Red Flags is too many Red Flags? Ideally just one. One should be enough. But girl, I get it. Sometimes to be sure, you need to collect two, three, five, ten until you have enough for a whole cheerleading squad. Give me a "T," give me an "O," give me an "X," give me an "I," give me a "C." What's that spell? The perfect guy for me!!!

And Red Flags can be easy to miss. Is he in love with me or love bombing me? Do I have butterflies because I have a crush or because I'm going to throw up? It feels the same!!!

Like Consultant Sam has a great job; he's a consultant. But when you think about it, that's a Red Flag. A man that you pay to tell you what to do? Guys will do that for free.

And Real Estate Sam? Well, he would vacillate between consistent and inconsistent communication, and I'd usually have to initiate. Red flag, but that was easy to miss because he was really hot. So. Anyway, kind of hard to ghost me when you're running the marathon. (I can track you in the app, bitch!)

I hope that by laying out all these Red Flags—almost one hundred of them! (Is that true? I can't count)—I'll save you some time and some STIs. While you bravely go out into the world and date, this book is here for you to rifle through before you put on a full face of war paint (makeup) and armor (sexy going-out top) and accept a drink from what could be the love of your life! Or a literal demon. Laugh, cry, commiserate, tally up your points, and learn from my mistakes . . . or don't, if the sex is really good.

Appearance Red Flags

Sometimes, you spot a Red Flag from a mile away with your own two eyes. Sometimes you even see them without your contacts in, because you had a one-night stand and forgot to pack your glasses for the next morning. (Oops.)

Toxicity is tied to appearance in nature ALL the damn time. It's called aposematism (okay, you learned something already!), and it's just science, babe. Poison dart frogs scream STAY THE FUCK AWAY, I'LL KILL YOU with their brightly colored skin. Puffer fish and porcupines have literal spikes. Fuckboys, well, they have sleeve tattoos and little hoop earrings to tell you they'll hurt you.

The flash of exposed ankle in the rolled-up pant leg, the five toes (or four toes, what happened to the pinky?) peeking out of a flip-flop at dinner. His appearance spells out LOSER on his forehead like a tattoo, and if he has that tattoo, well. He must have a huge penis; otherwise, how does he have the confidence to leave the house? Sometimes bad guys just LOOK bad, but amazing in leather.

MOM
A BOOK BY
ITS COVER
1

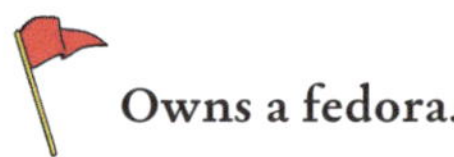

Owns a fedora.

Run.

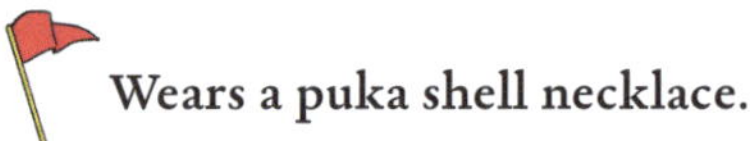

Wears a puka shell necklace.

Either he's just entered the villa, or he's going to act like he has and flirt with other bombshells.

Wears button-down shirts tucked into khakis with a nice pair of Merrells.

That's my dad. Or someone's dad. You're the Red Flag! Get away from him!

Has an eyebrow piercing and is pulling it off.

Yeah, they can get anyone they want.

Underdresses for every occasion.

Are you walking me down the aisle in jeans and backward sunglasses?!

Wears a blazer on a first date.

Is this a date or a business meeting?

Owns a lot of novelty T-shirts with "funny" expressions on them.

Childish? Yes, and . . . probably on an improv team.

Has a tattoo of an ex's name.

I was in a situationship with a guy who had his ex's initials tattooed on his thigh. OK, just two letters . . . no problem. He also wrote a one-man show about her . . . now we're talking a full script.

And he couldn't even text me back? Not even five words for me?!

If you guessed he didn't have a bed frame, you'd be right.

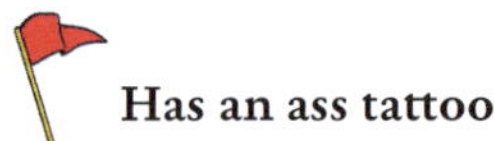

Has an ass tattoo.

Once, I went home with a guy and
when we took off our clothes, I realized
he had "sorry mom" tattooed.
On his left butt cheek.
In Helvetica.
So of course, I fucked him!

He then stood me up on our second date.
Hope he got "sorry jenny" tattooed
on the other cheek.

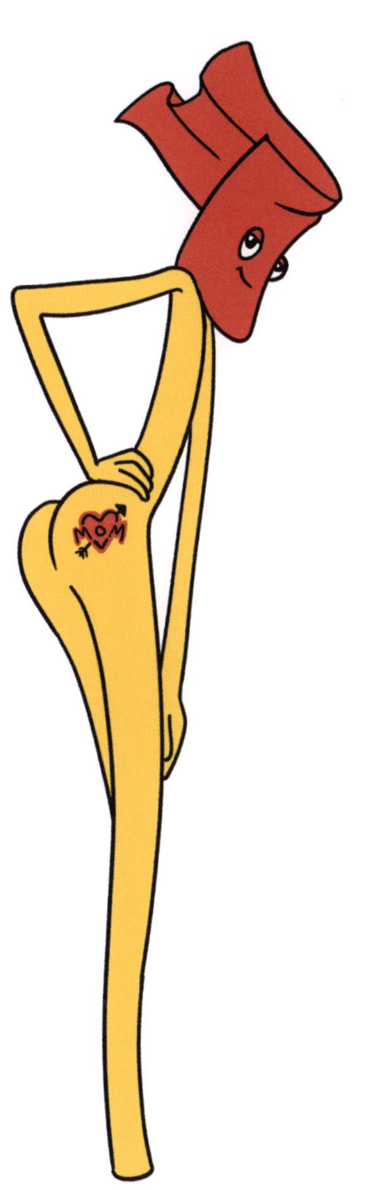
MOM

All of his underwear has holes.

Yuck. Grow up.

All of his underwear is from the same brand, fitted, sexy, and matches.

He knows too much. Who taught him?

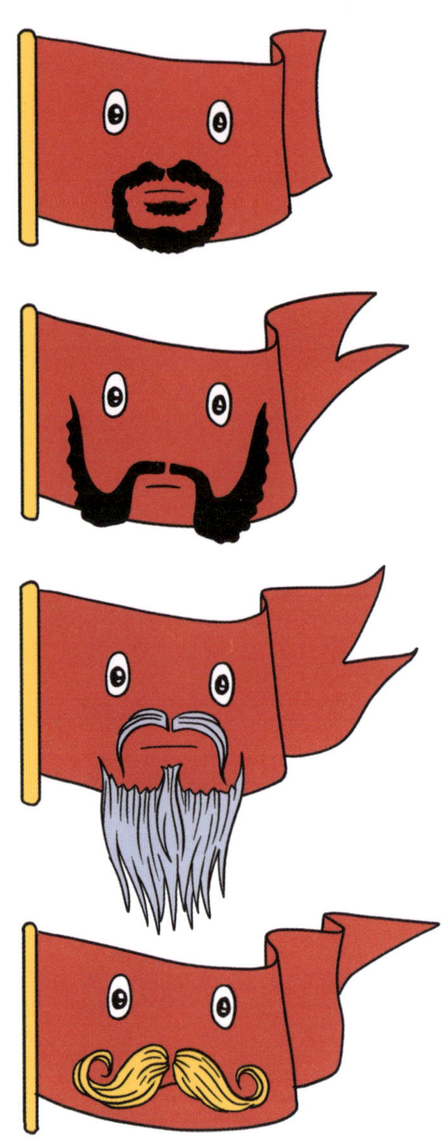

Maintains a goatee,

(Creepy)

mutton chops,

(Creepy)

Fu Manchu,

(Creepy AND *racist)*

or handlebar mustache with twisty ends.

(He's going to tie you to railroad tracks)

Is going bald, but in denial.

Shh, shh, it's going to be okay. Just shave it off.
. . . or let's vacation in Turkey!!

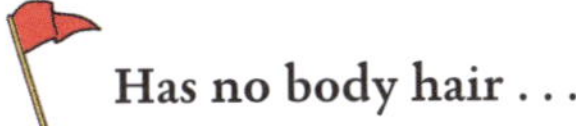

Has no body hair . . .

If he's not a professional swimmer (also a Red Flag, literally a slippery character), he's trying to not leave any evidence behind at the crime scene. Do a quick Google to look for a record and next time you're together, hold his hand . . . to check for fingerprints.

Dating App Red Flags

This is for the guys.

The dating app profile is *literally* a dating resume! If you handed a crumpled piece of paper with blurry headings and one-word summaries to a potential employer, do you think that will get you the job?! You have fifteen seconds to pique my interest and make me want to meet you IRL before I keep swiping.

An ideal dating app profile will give you some insight into their interests, occupation, social life, family, height, and whether they can catch a big fish. (Fingers crossed they caught a big fish.)

Sure, "we'll get along" if, "we get along," but that doesn't tell me anything about *you*, my dude. Out of all the guys in that massive group photo (Red Flag for that many dudes to hang out), which one are you?! And please to God list your real job. You don't actually work at Dunder Mifflin.

SWIPE LEFT
2
hey
heyy..
hey

Doesn't have any photos with friends.

I'm thinking he doesn't have any friends.

Only has selfies.

Not only does he not have friends . . . he doesn't know anyone.

Obstructs their face in every photo.

I went on a date with a guy who was wearing sunglasses in all of his photos.

Turns out he was a demon . . . JK.

His eyes were empty holes!! . . . JK.

He actually was kind of awkward and bad at eye contact.

Only has blurry photos.

That guy is either ugly, or he's really, really fast.

Has a photo holding a big fish.

If you want me to know you can provide, post a photo of your bank account.

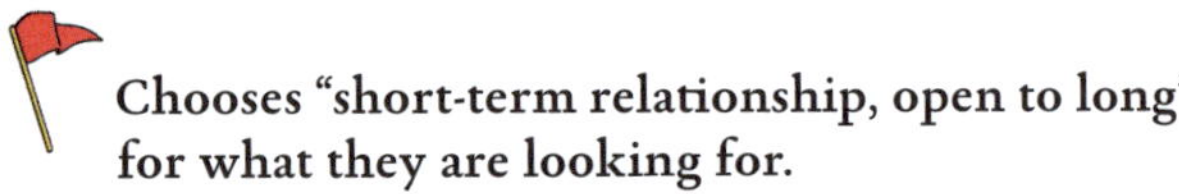

Chooses "short-term relationship, open to long" for what they are looking for.

You mean casual. We know.

Is "Moderate."

Pick a side.

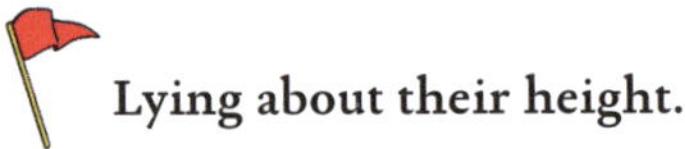

Lying about their height.

6'3"? Really? I'm bringing my tape measure.

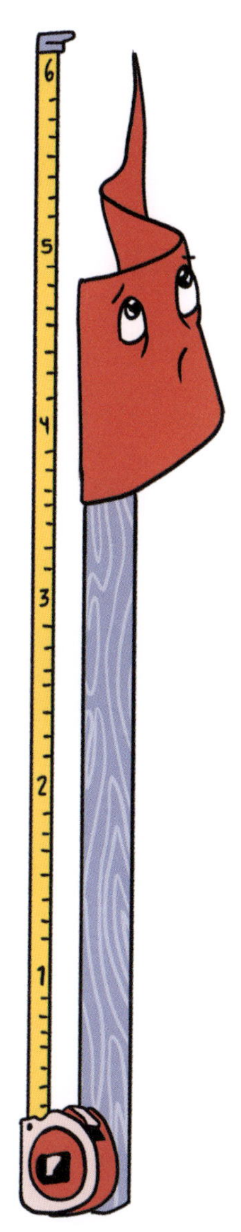
6
5
4
3
2
1

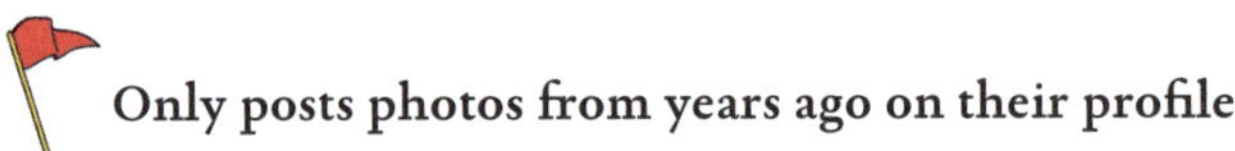

Only posts photos from years ago on their profile.

Did you time travel from the future to tell me not to go on this date?

Says "hey" as an opening line after matching.

Respond to ANYTHING on my profile.
Can you read?

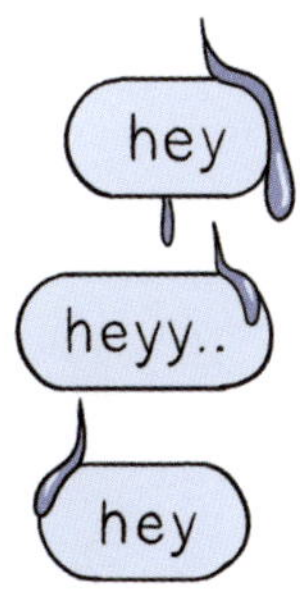

Answers the dating app prompts with the following:

"THE BEST WAY TO ASK ME OUT IS BY ASKING ME OUT."
No, YOU ask ME out.

"I'M AMAZING AT GETTING MY HOODIE BACK."
The least you could do is let us keep the hoodie. I'm freezing. Jesus Christ.

"WHAT I ORDER FOR THE TABLE—GUACAMOLE."
Tell me less about you.
Oh, let me guess, you also have a mom and a dad? Five fingers? Are breathing???

"BIGGEST RISK: DOWNLOADING THIS APP."
Charmed life you're living, Brian.

"LET'S AGREE ON A LIE ABOUT HOW WE MET."
At this point it's a legitimate miracle if we met on an app. We should tell the Pope.

"TYPICAL SUNDAY: FOOTBALL."
Great. That's awesome. Can't wait for you to watch the game on your iPad when we go out to dinner on the LORD'S DAY.

"I'M OVERLY COMPETITIVE ABOUT EVERYTHING."
Relax.

"I'LL FALL FOR YOU, IF YOU TRIP ME."
What if I punch you in the face instead?

Still has the apps downloaded after we're dating.

I'm right here!!!!!!!!!!!!!!!!!!!!!!!!!!!!!!!!!!!

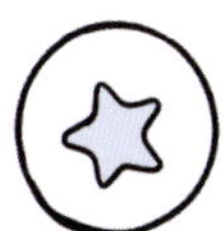

Online Red Flags

Our ancestors woke up at the crack of dawn. Milked the cows. Carried pails of milk to boil and then wore out their arms churning butter. Now, we wake up to see who liked our posts. If my crush isn't liking them, I'm not getting out of bed!! What's the point?!

My screen time is no fewer than twelve hours a day, and more than half of those hours are spent stalking potential romantic partners (Andrew Garfield is a potential romantic partner even if he doesn't know it yet). The other five are spent watching videos of funny cats.

Since we're interacting with our phones more than we are with people (It's dystopian, but Katniss had TWO love interests at least. So, doesn't sound that bad to me!), you need to be on the alert for behaviors that warrant the red alarm emoji. If he acts like an ass online, you better believe he'll be one IRL. For breaking my community guidelines, you're blocked!

STOP,
DROP,
AND SCROLL
3
0
1
2
1
1

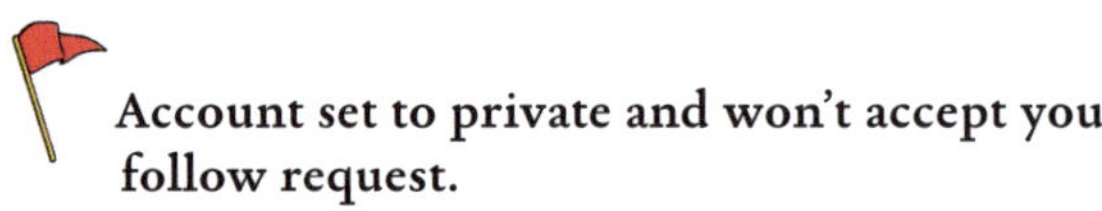

Account set to private and won't accept your follow request.

I'll show you a Woman In STEM. Girls, we're hacking into the mainframe.

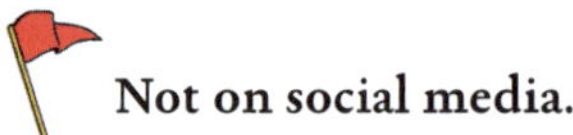

Not on social media.

What year is it? Who is the president?
Where does he get his news? His recipes?
His celebrity gossip? His videos of teens doing little dances they made up? Or funny cats?
His information in general? An almanac?!
Oh my god.
He might be in a coma.

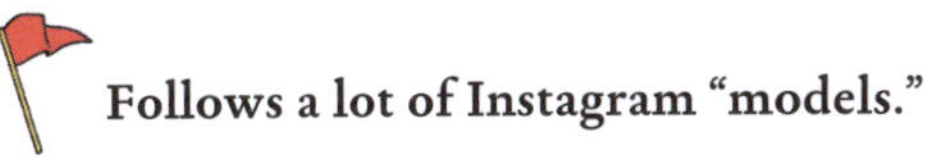

Follows a lot of Instagram "models."

It's not for the captions!

Only posts thirst traps.

I hate to break it to you, but this relationship might be a trap!!

Comments flirty things on other girls' posts.

Using the heart-eye emoji IS cheating!

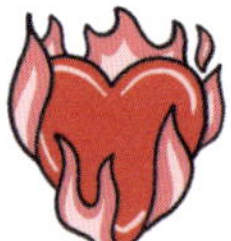

Refuses to learn to take good pictures of you.

It's not that hard. Flip your method for taking pictures with your method for fingering.

The slow, constantly checking in, careful, swiping up a little bit, then down for another angle.
"Do you like this?"
"How is this?"
"Is this good for you?"
(That's actually for fingering.)

And then blasting that button like you're trying to get kills in a video game:
"Fuck yeah!"
"Hell Yeah!"
"Let's Go!!"
(That one is for your Instagram Boyfriend.)

#ramen #noods #foodie

Never posts pictures of you on their profile.

Look, I get that an aesthetic photo of your dinner is sick, or whatever, but what about the beautiful girl you just ate dinner with? What about her?!

Never likes your posts.

If you don't like my content, do you even like me?!

Constantly sends fire reactions to your stories.

Hate to break it to you, but he's sending them to everyone . . . And I'll show him a fire IRL when I burn down his house.

ONLY flirts in memes.

You know the one where the dog is sitting and the house is on fire around him, and he's like, "everything's fine"?
Yeah . . . That's how you're making me feel.
Did that get through to you!?

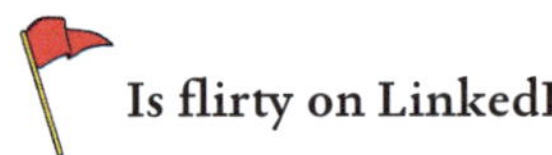

Is flirty on LinkedIn.

I lost touch with the guy I lost my virginity to
until he sent me a connection request
ON LINKEDIN.
In the picture, he's wearing a suit and sunglasses
and is standing in front of a convertible.
Like a fuckboy . . . professionally.
Should I endorse him for conciseness and
brevity? (He lasted three minutes.)

Has zero followers.

Call the police, you caught a serial killer.

Has millions of followers.

Call the police, you found a narcissist.

Is active on Facebook.

Don't ask him his thoughts on the moon landing.

Is active on Snapchat.

Double-check he's not using a fake ID.

Still Venmo-ing his ex for things.

It's not over!

Sends you Venmo requests for everything.

No, I will not be paying for half.
My presence is priceless, I should be sending you an invoice.

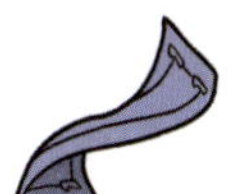

On-the-Date Red Flags

We're doing it! We're meeting face-to-face at an establishment and asking each other the tough questions! *"How many siblings do you have?" "What do your parents do?" "Did you watch* Game of Thrones*?"*

It's like Einstein said (yeah, I'm quoting Einstein, bitch): "A good date feels like only a minute."

Then somehow, you've had three drinks? Gone to multiple locations? Are making out on the street? Wait, we are at the apartment now? How did that happen?!

But a bad date, one minute feels like nine thousand hours. How fast can I slurp down this spicy marg and bounce? Can I tell him I've just been in an accident and I have to leave when I've been sitting across from him the whole time?

CHECK PLEASE!
4

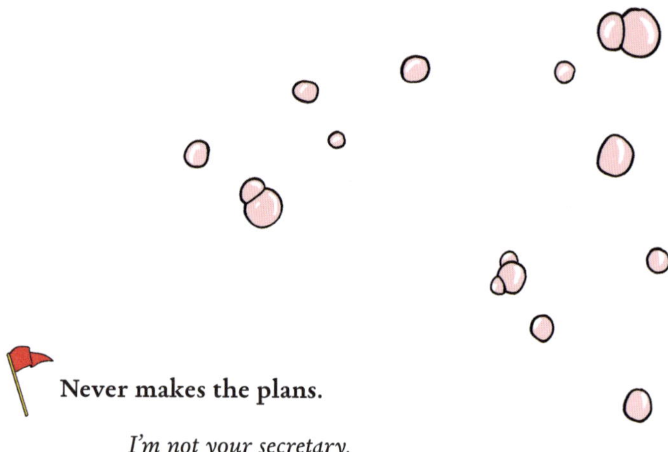

Never makes the plans.

I'm not your secretary.

Arrives late.

Is my time not important to you? That being said, I'm going to be ten minutes late.

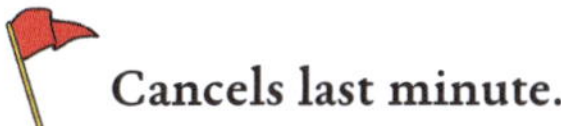

Cancels last minute.

Just rude! But I am a little relieved and putting on sweats. Thank you, and you're a dick!

Chooses a venue really close to their home for a first date.

That's a little presumptuous, sir . . .

Wait, the venue . . . is their apartment?

Sir, that's presumptuous AND sketchy. Either he's broke or wants to chop you up and keep you in the fridge. Not sure which is worse.

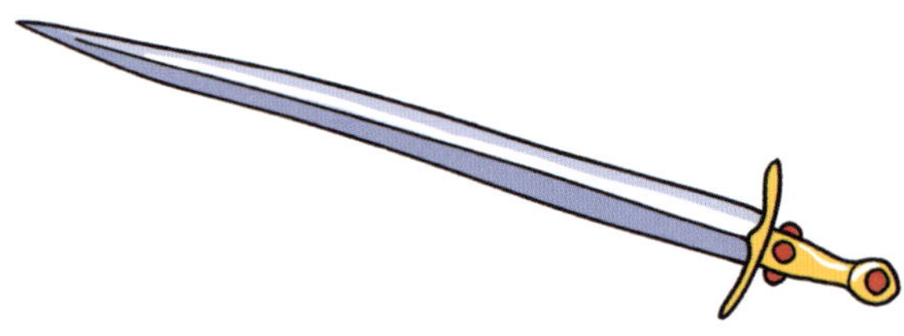

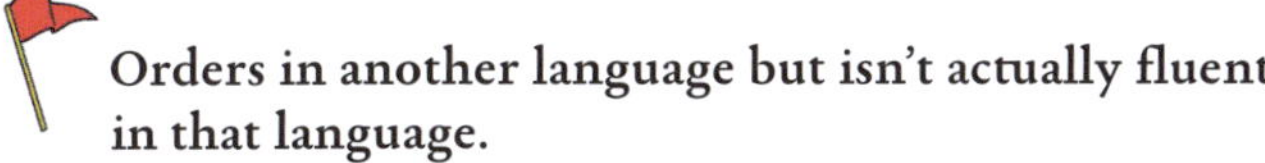

Orders in another language but isn't actually fluent in that language.

Cómo se dice . . . ew?

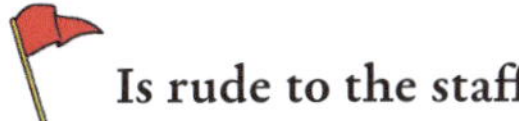

Is rude to the staff.

I mean. Feels obvious.

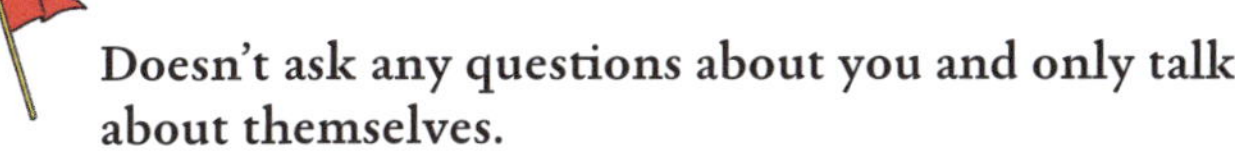

Doesn't ask any questions about you and only talk about themselves.

I could watch a TED Talk instead and learn something, asshole.

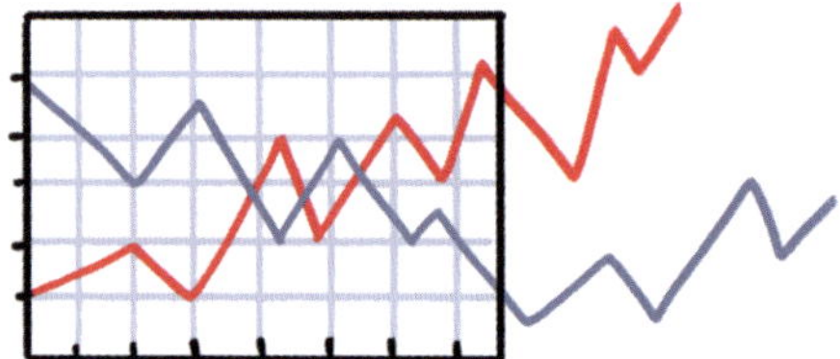

Explains the stock market to you over drinks.

The stock market isn't real. Someone made it up.
It's like explaining the plot of The Lord of the Rings.
Come to think of it . . . don't do that either.

Way outpaces you in drinks.

I went on a date where he downed five beers in the amount of time it took me to drink one glass of rosé.
Didn't realize he was a freshman pledging a fraternity. I'm not making you chug . . .
I'm not Sigma Chi.

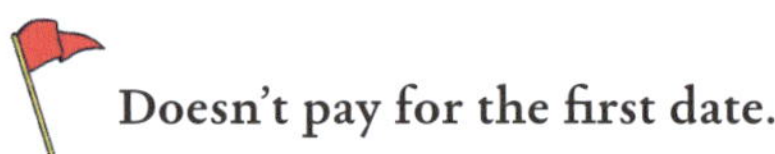

Doesn't pay for the first date.

Look, I'm going to reach in the general direction of my purse, but we all know that's just an interpretive dance.

Texting throughout the whole movie.

Pretty sure the video going around your group chat isn't a cinematic masterpiece.

Only ever wants to Netflix and Chill.

Watching TV at home is not a date! Especially if we're watching on your parent's account. Wait, it's your ex's!?

Not available during the day, but always available at night.

If you're going to act like a vampire, then vampire rules apply, and I don't invite you inside me or my house! Scram!

Occupation Red Flags

When a guy is gainfully employed, that's a Green Flag. Baseline, he needs to have a source of income because you and I both know that money is, BY DESIGN, a little green flag. The mint decided to make it green!

And when he's passionate about his work, good at his job, and able to set healthy boundaries with his workplace? Even better! Definitely link up with a guy with a good LinkedIn. But sometimes his work just isn't going to work for you.

IT'S NOT WORKING
5

Being an amateur magician.

Please.
He spent hours practicing card tricks alone in his room . . . for fun?

Being a professional magician.

[Although that's kind of sexy.]
[. . . fuck]

Does stand-up comedy.

Working out your baggage onstage doesn't count. Try therapy instead.

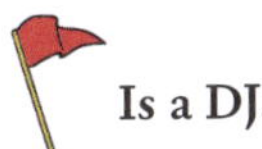

Is a DJ.

Need I say more?

Has competed or applied to be on *The Bachelorette*.

No way he's here for the right reasons.

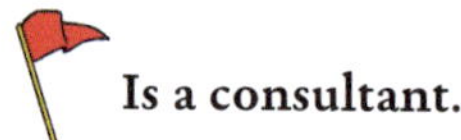

Is a consultant.

A man that's paid to tell you what to do?
He'll do that for free.

Back to Consultant Sam:
On our second date, he asked, "what are we doing?"
I said, "Going on one date a week . . . "
Do you need a strategic plan for where the relationship is going? Do you want a deck?
Is this timeline not working for your critical path to reach our goal of a long-term relationship?
You're not going to hit your quarterly KPIs with that attitude.
Do you not see the potential for a huge ROI if we keep seeing each other?
Take this offline and ping me after you've gotten your ducks in a row to align on where this is going.
Circling back, why are we talking about this after having dinner and seeing a movie? We needed this deliverable before EOD.
Actually, let's table this until after we have sex.
Because I'm not wearing any pants.
Oh, we've reached the hard stop for this meeting?
Well, I want a reimbursement for my car home.

Is a male therapist . . . to women.

A job in mansplaining . . .

In one of their sessions, my friend's male therapist taught her "W.A.I.T."
Why
Am
I
Talking?

He said she tended to overshare . . .
I think he tended to silence women.

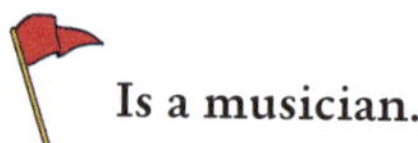

Is a musician.

Always "on tour." You're avoiding me.

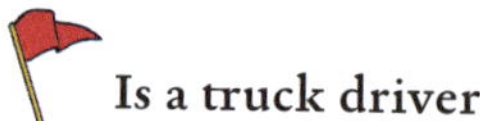

Is a truck driver.

Always "driving cross-country." Okay, you hate me.

Is a pilot.

Oh, you hate me so much you take to the SKIES!

Is an astronaut.

That's so mean.

Is "between jobs" for months.

He's just unemployed, babe. He's not paying for this cocktail.

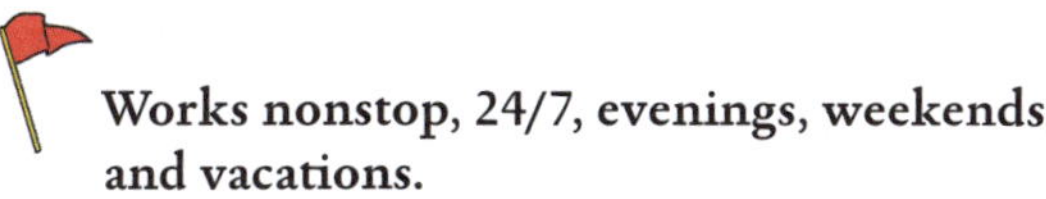

Works nonstop, 24/7, evenings, weekends, and vacations.

Are you dating me or your boss?

Doesn't have to work because of generational wealth.

That one is mine. Back off.

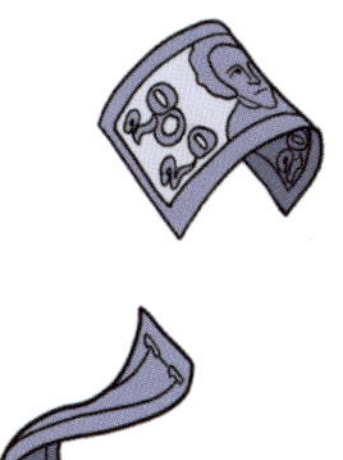

Hobby Red Flags

You are what you do.
I'm pretty sure Buddha said that.
Some hobbies are delightful:
cooking, fostering kittens, and
volunteering for the community.

Some are making and flying model
planes, which means you'll spend many
afternoons standing in a hot parking lot,
watching them fly them. And no, you're
not allowed to fly the plane because
you'll probably crash it.

HE IS WHAT HE DOES
6
SPORTS

Is waaaaaaay too into working out.

No, I don't want to go on a "run." No man is worth running for unless he's trying to murder me.

Is always running marathons.

What are you running from?

Is into parkour.

There is something called the sidewalk that works just fine.

Is learning how to breakdance.

I don't want to see that. No one needs to see that. You should keep something to yourself.

Is *extremely* into gaming.

Let me put it in terms you can understand: Our relationship is going to take a hit, and your health bar is gonna go down, and you're losing points with me if you don't turn it off.

Whole personality is a sports team.

No, you can't have your iPad out to watch the game at dinner.

Drinks full glasses of milk.

It's just unsettling. Something does not sit right . . . It's even weird when Santa does it.

Is a Disney adult.

Grow up.

Is a film guy.

I don't need you to mansplain Dune *to me.*

Goes to Paris alone.

My ex-boyfriend went to Paris "to find himself," and somehow "found" a hot French girl. I should have known; no man goes to Paris by himself.

Is all about spontaneous travel.

Everyone's "spontaneously flown to Bali." That's not a personality. That's a mental breakdown.

Parties all the time.

I'm so sleepy. Can we please go to bed?

Never wants to go out.

Let me shake my ass for once.

Never likes to spend any money.

If we do one more frozen food date night, I will scream! Take me to dinner!

Loves loves loves to spend lots of money.

Unless he's a billionaire, which is also a Red Flag. But I don't mind a Red Flag if it's hoisted from a yacht.

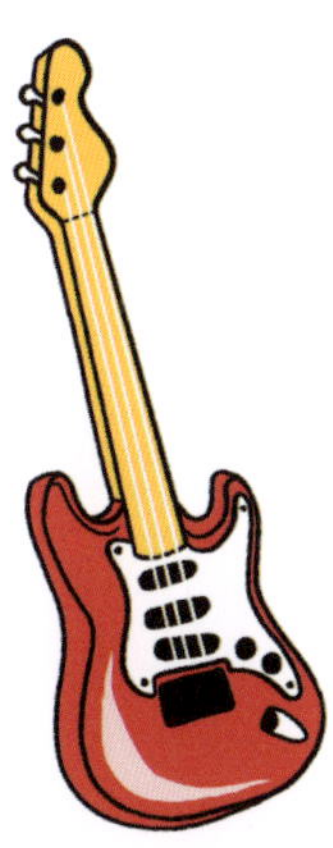

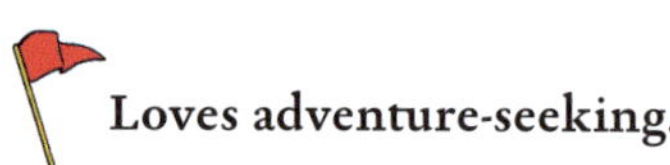

Loves adventure-seeking.

Look, I tried waterfall jumping. I got an ear infection immediately upon impact. That's not a vacation. That's a death wish.

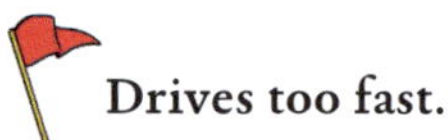

Drives too fast.

YOU'RE NOT IN THE FAST & FURIOUS *MOVIES!*

Home Red Flags

No need to go to a haunted house in October,
just step inside a single man's apartment,
and it's enough to give you the heebie-jeebies.
It sends a shiver down my spine when I see
the inexplicable stains in the bathroom (ah!),
the dying plants (no!), the bed on the floor!!!!!!!
(AHHHHHHHHHH!)

And the state of his towel? Babe, that's
a jump scare. The right guy's digs will feel
like a home away from home. The wrong
guy's will feel like you've fallen into a hole.

HOME IS
WHERE THE
RED FLAG IS
7
3
IN
1

Has a sword on display.

That's . . . cool? How do you want me to react? Did you . . . buy it . . . online?

Or was it gifted to you . . . by a mentor? Um. I don't know if it is better or worse if you know how to use it.

Clown-related décor.

Of course! Of course! It doesn't matter how "hot" or "nice" or how "good" the sex is. Get the fuck out of there.

Lots of pictures of themself on their walls.

Did his mom decorate?

Only has beer and condiments in the fridge.

*Not even one vegetable? He has scurvy.
And maybe rabies. Definitely HPV.*

Uses 3-in-1 Shampoo, Conditioner, Body Wash.

That stuff is probably toxic, right?

Only owns one towel.

If we're dating, we're each going to need a towel. We're not going to share. You need at least four. And, get this: washcloths.

PINK FLOYD

Doesn't have a bed frame.

We're not sleeping on THE FLOOR or YOUR COUCH or THE DOG BED. We're not pets!

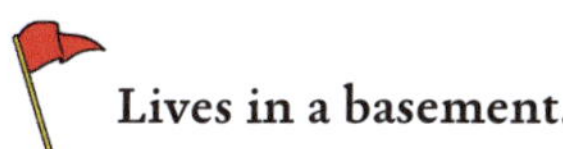

Lives in a basement.

We need a window.

Not knowing what a top sheet is!

GET A FUCKING TOP SHEET! IT'S THE SHEET THAT GOES . . . ON TOP! Please! I'm begging.

Not knowing how to fold a fitted sheet.

That is what YouTube is for.

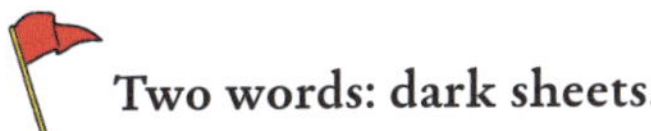

Two words: dark sheets.

Listen to me; if his sheets are a dark color, they've never been washed.

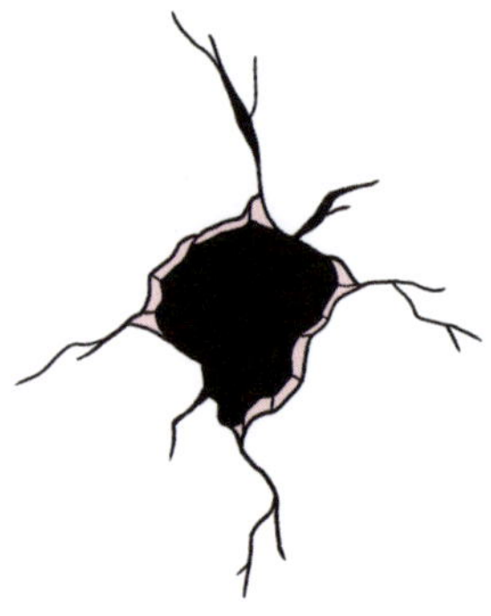

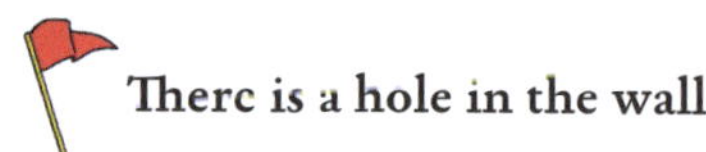

There is a hole in the wall.

If that's how you're gonna react, you're gonna have to get a little handier. Spackle that shit.

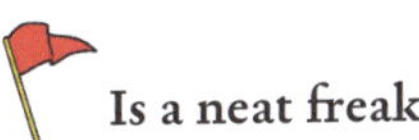

Is a neat freak.

A man once yelled at me for spilling on his couch . . .

Literally me or the couch?

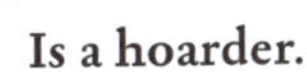

Is a hoarder.

If I can't see the floor, we can't do this.

Lives with more than two roommates.

That's legally a fraternity . . . or for girls, a coven.

Has a female roommate . . . that is also his ex.

Don't worry about her, babe, we just LIVE together. We're just LOOKING AT APARTMENTS! We're just negotiating BROKER'S FEES! We're just picking out a COUCH! No worries.

Communication Red Flags

"U up?"
Yes, I can't sleep because I'm having nightmares
about Sam who texted me daily then
disappeared for a week. Then said he wasn't
ghosting me when I called him out on it.

Then a week later said, "I don't think
we're a good match." WHY DIDN'T YOU
JUST SAY THAT THE FIRST TIME?!

So yes, I'm "up," thanks for asking!
Is it really that hard to respond in a timely manner?
Say what you're feeling!
"I love you" is only three words!
None are more than one syllable.

TOXIC
IN THE
TEXT BUBBLES
8
I love you
Read 12:31 am
U up?

Being under twenty-six years old.

His prefrontal cortex isn't fully developed. It's still goop in there. His brain is a runny egg, and you deserve an omelet, babe.

Uses start-up language when flirting.

No, we're not going to circle back, and no, I don't want to put a pin in this. Guess I won't see you for the quarter! It's time to set a kill date on this relationship.

 **Not replying to a text for over a day.**

 **Not replying to a text for over 12 hours.**

 **Not replying to a text for over 6 hours.**

 **Not replying to a text for over 3 hours.**

 **Actually, not replying to a text within minutes.**

No one is that busy!

 **Texts you 24/7.**

Needy much? I'm busy . . . looking at my phone.

1. **Leaving the read receipts on.**

2. **Reading a text.**

3. **Not replying.**

You're a psychopath and need to be locked up for the good of society.

Is super communicative and then super uncommunicative.

Like when it's on, oh it's on, when it's off, you're like what the fuck happened?

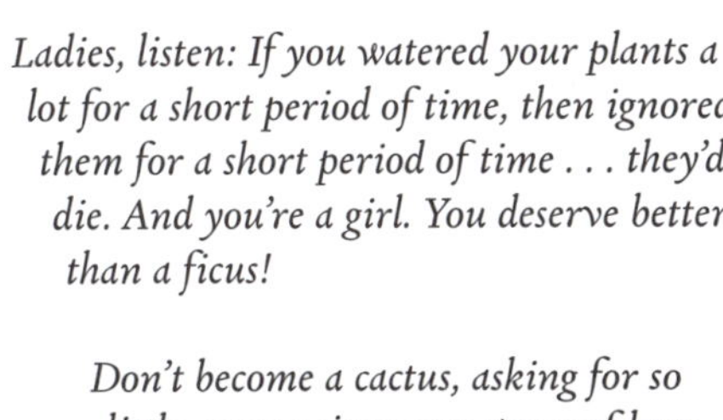

Ladies, listen: If you watered your plants a lot for a short period of time, then ignored them for a short period of time . . . they'd die. And you're a girl. You deserve better than a ficus!

Don't become a cactus, asking for so little, conserving your stores of love and affection from the last time it rained, even if that was days, weeks, months ago. And again, you're a GIRL!

Instead, be a fiddle-leaf fig. If you don't water me exactly how I want, when I want, then it's OVER. I'm fucking done, bitch.

Bringing up their ex in conversation . . . All. The. Time.

Look, I love her, respect her, and thank her for all she's done to make him a better man, but . . . what the fuck is happening here!? It can't be anything good.

Interrupts or talks over you.

Silencing a woman. I don't think so.

Always nagging you.

If I wanted to feel just a little bit bad about myself, I'd call my mom. Thanks.

Doesn't show interest in your hobbies.

It's always "watching the game" and never "eating charcuterie and doing our nails." Maybe you'd like it!

Always starting fights.

You wanna go? Mentally, you're playing slaps, and I'm doing Krav Maga.

Uses pet names immediately.

Did you forget my name?

Forgets important details.

You should be ready at any moment for a pop quiz. What's my middle name? Clock is ticking . . .

Always canceling plans.

He's just not that into you! His grandma can't die more than twice!

Controlling what you do, who you see, what you wear, what you eat, or like, of literally anything.

Did I ask for your opinion?

Immediately tells you they're really into you; gives a ton of compliments, and gifts, and attention.

Let's call in the dogs. We've got a love bomb threat on our hands, and the situationship might explode.

Sex Red Flags

Sexy time can quickly go from feeling very hot and bothered to just feeling hot, as in heated, as in actually bothered. In the blink of an eye that has been staring straight into my soul the entire time we've been hooking up, the make-out can quickly turn to get out. I have gotten the ick. What are you starting at? Do I have something in my teeth?

We're all searching for the "G-Spot," and by that I mean Green Flag, of course. When it comes to sex, it's the four C's: Consent, Communication, Caring, and . . . Clitoris. It's about BOTH of your pleasures (I mean, mostly yours first, please), and your partner should be hyper-focused on giving you exactly what you want. And making it feel fun and not at all embarrassing, even though it's vulnerable. You're laid bare. Literally.

With the wrong person, you're like "oh my god, what the fuck" and with the right one, you're like "oh my god, oh my god, oh my god, fuck, fuck, fuck." Does that track?

HOT AND
ACTUALLY
BOTHERED
9
03:00:00

Doesn't respond excitedly to your nudes or your naked body.

I'm gonna need a full AWOOOOGA!
Holy shit!
Thank you, God, for all my blessings! (He was an atheist before, now he has found religion.)
Eyes rolled back in the head.
Faint!
Have a literal heart attack, or I don't want it.

Doesn't keep your nudes in a safe place.

Be careful!!! Don't let those get in the wrong hands!
Hello?! I could charge money for those!

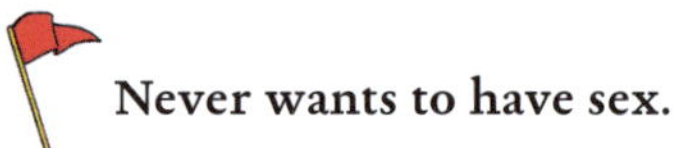

Never wants to have sex.

Look, I have needs!

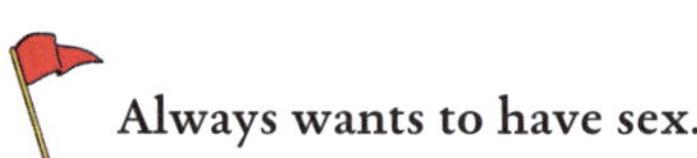

Always wants to have sex.

And I need a break!

 **Insists on sex on the first date.**

I'm a lady!

But I did have two glasses of rosé . . .
Okay, I'm down.

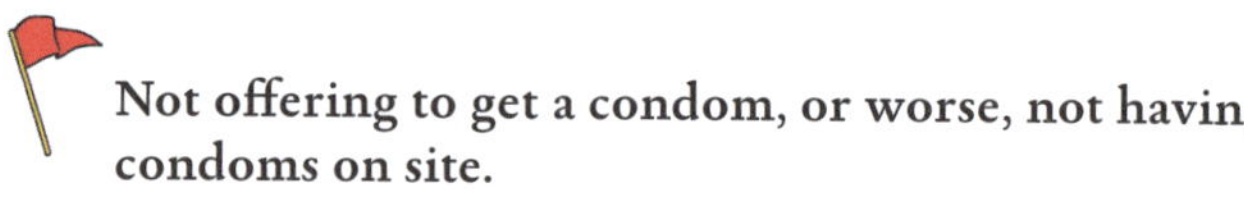

Not offering to get a condom, or worse, not having condoms on site.

Safety first. Also, I don't know what size you are.

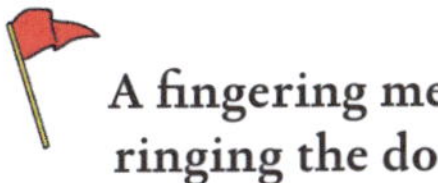

A fingering method that could be compared to ringing the doorbell over and over again.

No one is cumming for you.

Doggy-style every time.

What's wrong with my face?!

Missionary every time.

Yawn. I think I'll just take a nap during.

Cums and then doesn't at least try to return the favor.

Selfish!!!! Did your mother not teach you manners?

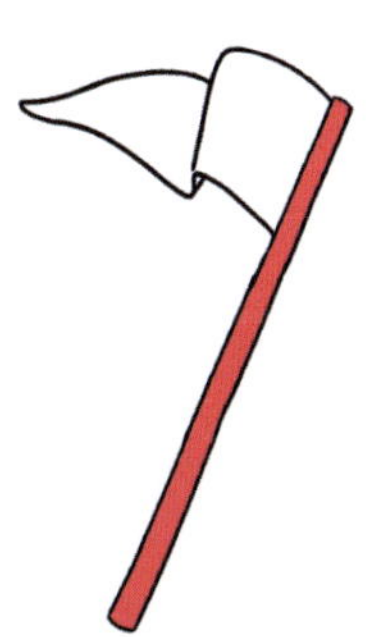

Looks down on your fantasies.

I didn't say anything about your Legend of Zelda *thing!*

Never goes down on you.

Excuse me, you need your daily protein intake, sir.

Is emasculated by your vibrator.

If LeBron James was on your team, would you be mad that he scored more points than you? Or would you be happy that you won? He dunked, and you made an assist. That's an alley-oop. Teamwork.

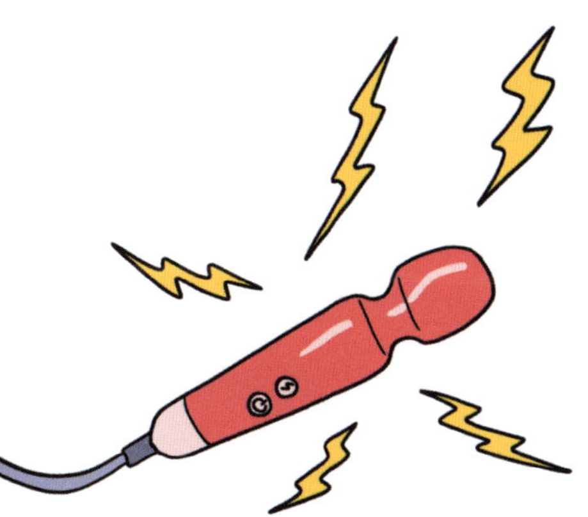

Not bringing me a glass of water after banging.

What, do you want me to die of thirst? Is this The Hunger Games?

Finishes in three minutes.

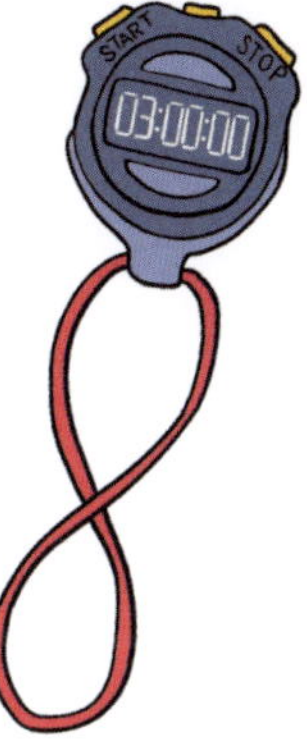

Finishes in three hours.

Past Relationship Red Flags

Every girl leaves her ex a little better for the person who comes next. It's like the Boy Scout Rule: Leave it better than you found it.

Leave it knowing how to buy flowers, give compliments, or put the seat down at the very least. And I'm grateful to all of the exes that came before me for the hard work that they put in. Unfortunately, sometimes, how you found it can be a field full of loose garbage set on literal fire, no offense.

BATTLE OF THE EXES
10

Has never had a serious relationship.

Not gonna start now.

Always in and out of serious relationships.

Have you tried dating yourself?

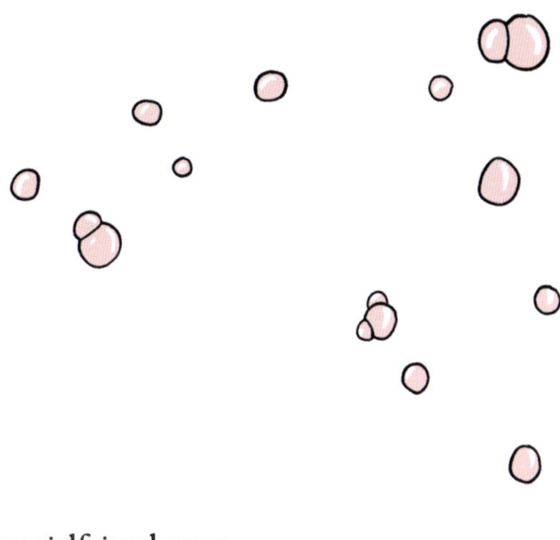

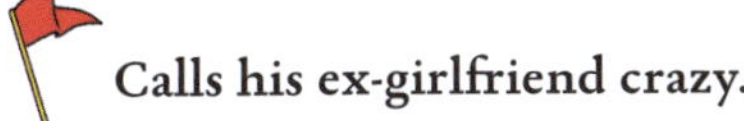

Calls his ex-girlfriend crazy.

She's not crazy. You made her crazy.

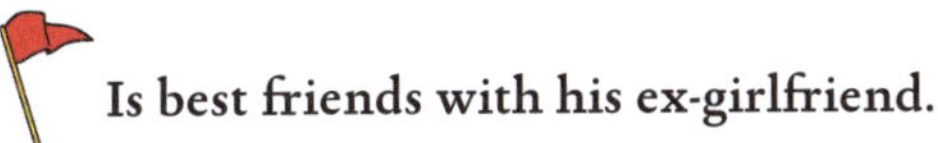

Is best friends with his ex-girlfriend.

History famously repeats itself. And he's gonna repeat himself all the way back to her.

Is always on and off with his ex-girlfriend.

I was obsessed with this guy who was still texting his ex, who he had been long-distance with for years before we dated. They had always been long-distance and on and off.
And while they were off, we were on.

I cried a Pacific Ocean (where his ex lives) and an Atlantic Ocean (where I live) worth of tears over him in the span of a few months while we were in this intense situationship.

He then went on a break with me to get back with her. It was never MY break; it was always HER break.

If you feel like you're the other woman in someone else's love story . . . you probably are.

Is 37+ and has never married.

Why? I'm scared.

Recently separated.

Is it a year? A month? A week? Gonna need that paperwork to go through before we can make an appointment.

Recently divorced.

He's 17 again. And not in the hot Zac Efron way.

His ex posted that he's a psychopath.

I met a hot guy, so naturally, I looked him up online.
Found his marriage license. Then his divorce filing.

His Instagram . . . private.
His ex-wife's Instagram . . . public.

In her most recent post, she said that she was happy to be out of her marriage and used the hashtag #pyschopath. It was so bad she made it a hashtag.

Yeah, I'm gonna believe women on this one.

Family & Friends Red Flags

You are who you surround yourself with. I'm pretty sure God said that. And it's true. If you are hanging in a swamp with swamp creatures, you're probably a swamp creature. (But Shrek is kind of hot so . . .)

The people you spend time with influence your thoughts, feelings, and how you see the world. If his friend group is fratty, messy, and breaking girls' hearts left and right? Honey, herd mentality. You'll get eaten up, spit out with nothing left on the bone (goal weight! JK!!).

And don't get me started on his family. We'll need to hire a professional for that . . .

HE IS WHO
HE HANGS WITH
11

Always prioritizing hanging with the buddies over you.

You're telling me you'd rather be in a big empty field, hitting balls toward a hole, in silence, for twelve hours than spend time with me? Sounds like biblical torture.

All his friends are single.

There might be something in the water . . . sorry, the Mountain Dew.

Their friends tell you not to date them.

One time I went over to a guy's apartment and realized he was roommates with an acquaintance of mine!

Hell yes! To wake up in the morning and get to gab with my girl . . . a dream come true.

Until she silently mouthed to me like an old man at a gas station in a horror movie:
"get the fuck out"
"go"
"leave while you still can"
"it's not safe here"

I didn't stay to find out what his demons were.

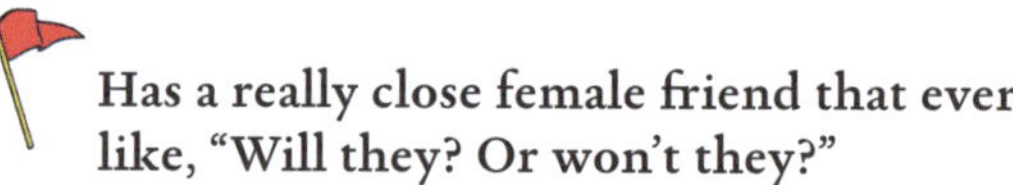

Has a really close female friend that everyone is like, "Will they? Or won't they?"

They will! Eventually, they will!

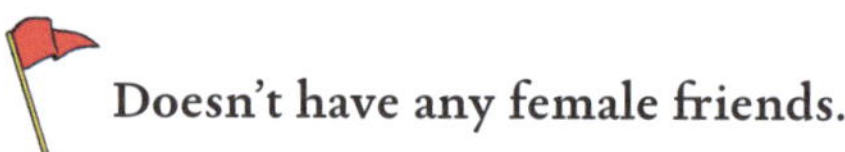

Doesn't have any female friends.

The friend group needs to pass the Bechdel test.

Won't introduce you to their friends and family.

What is he hiding?
Another girlfriend?

Another wife?
. . . and 2.5 kids?

He's a masked vigilante?!

Still lives at home.

When he finally moves out, you're his new mommy! You're having a boy! Congratulations!!!

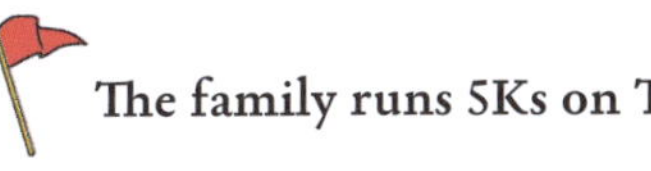

The family runs 5Ks on Thanksgiving.

I'm running in the other direction.

Being an only child.

Sorry to the only children, but you guys are freaks.

You don't know how to share.

You don't know how to communicate.

You learned card tricks alone in your room instead of becoming a person.

(The card tricks are pretty cool, though.)

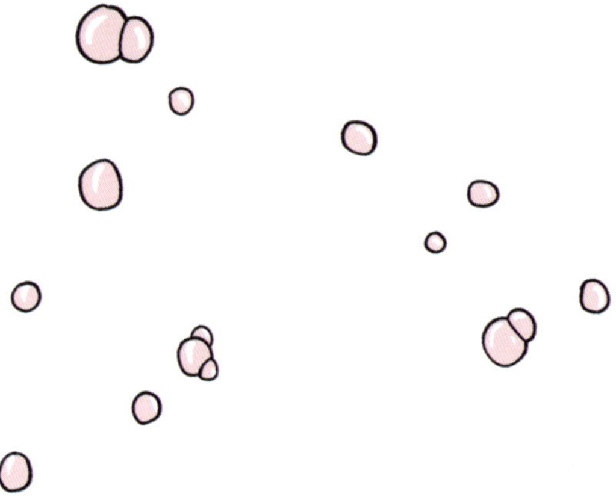

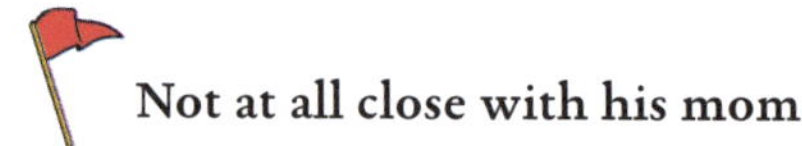

Not at all close with his mom.

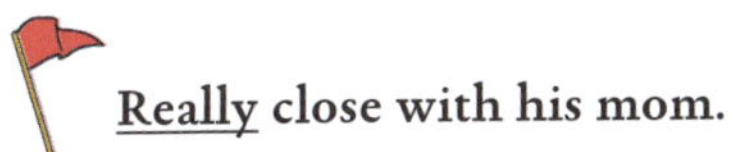

Really close with his mom.

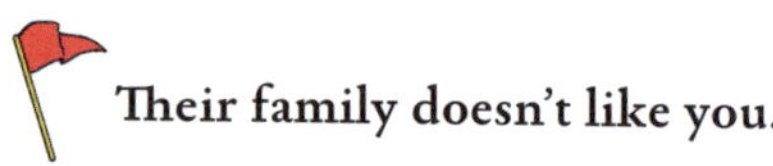

Their family doesn't like you.

Respectfully, fuck you, guys. Except for Christmas. But next year, we're going on a cruise.

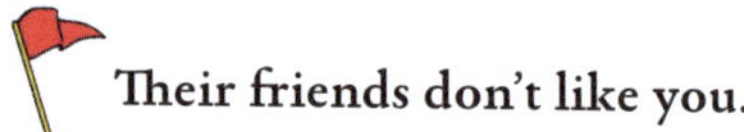

Their friends don't like you.

No problem, more space at the wedding.

HEY! WAIT A SECOND!!!!

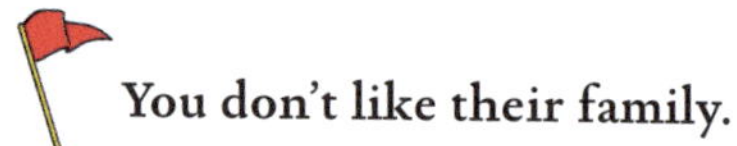

You don't like their family.

That's a lot of holidays. Forever . . .

You don't like their friends.

No problem, more space at the wedding.

FLIP IT AND REVERSE IT!

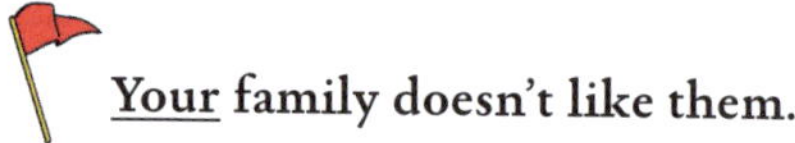

Your family doesn't like them.

Mother usually knows best, except that one time she said you'd look good with bangs.

<u>Your</u> friends don't like them.

Let's be real, boyfriends come and go, but friendship never ends, zigga zig ah.

Their family *really* likes you. Like too much. Like they're *really* excited.

He's never brought a girlfriend home before? No kidding. That's . . . awesome?

Afterword

WOW, I THINK THAT WAS ALMOST ONE HUNDRED RED FLAGS! (Was it? I still can't count. If you're a hot, single accountant, please get in touch to let me know.) As you move forward on your dating journey, I hope you feel better equipped to spot Red Flags in the wild. And it won't always be as cut-and-dry as my pussy when a man told me I was not his number one crush while he was inside of me. Keep that to yourself! Radical honesty is sometimes rude.

And unfortunately, sometimes a Red Flag for someone might be a Green Flag for someone else! One guy who has his ex's initials tattooed on him might still be into his ex (and even worse . . . a stand-up comedian). Or she might have died and he's keeping her memory alive, which actually makes him . . . sexy. Like almost a widower, which we all know is HOT.

Be vigilant, be brave, and stay safe out there. Listen to your gut. If it seems like a Red Flag, it probably is. Sent a cute text and haven't heard back for hours or days? Yeah, those aren't butterflies; that's a panic attack.

And most importantly, take care of yourself. You are so worth the best possible treatment from the people who are lucky enough to be liked or even loved by you. And looking for your person is vulnerable, scary, and requires SOOO much effort when you could have been watching TV in your sweats! I'm proud of you for putting on pants and TRYING.

Most of these people don't deserve your tears, let alone your sweetness or your shapewear! I'm sorry you ever got hurt.

And it was never your fault. It's always theirs. Is that toxic? Sure, we're allowed to have our own Red Flags. Love you!

Acknowledgments

I'D LIKE TO THANK MY TEAM AT RIZZOLI UNIVERSE, Jessica Fuller, and Sarah M. Sutherland, for entrusting me to write my first book. It's because of you I can now say I'm an author, and I'll never shut up about that for the rest of my life. I'm so thankful, not only for plucking me from the Internet but also for the care and consideration that went into the edit and how much fun it's been to commiserate about our bad dates.

I'm so grateful for the gorgeous illustrations from my longtime Internet crush, Margalit Cutler. You truly brought my ideas to life. And for the amazing work by our genius designer Kayleigh Jankowski, without whom this would just be a Word doc.

Thank you to my manager, Matt Fechter, one of the few men I know who is truly one of the good ones. Thanks for believing in me and my writing and, more importantly, being a wife guy (Green Flag). It's an honor and a privilege to do my part to contribute to your son Keanu's college fund. Thankfully, because he is a baby, he has yet to exhibit any Red Flags . . . for now.

I must acknowledge the team at the *New York Times*'s *Modern Love*, Dan Jones and Miya Lee, and my editor at *Cosmopolitan*, Madeleine Reeves. You were the first to take me seriously as a writer, even before I took myself seriously. I'm so unbelievably grateful. And look, I wrote a book! You did this! If anyone is offended by anything I wrote, blame them.

I'm so lucky for my incredible friends who have been there for me through all my dating woes, usually with a glass (just kidding, a whole bottle) of rosé. Without you, I wouldn't have known what to text my crush or which nude to send. I can't name you all because I will forget someone, and it'll be in print forever, and I'll feel so shitty about it and never sleep again. But know that I love you, and I'll sign a copy for you to put in your bathroom.

Thank you to my therapist, Hayley, who has spent years trying to keep me away from the guys I've written about here. Unfortunately, it's telehealth, and there isn't much you can do to stop me.

Thank you to my family, my dad, Alice, and Jacob, for all your support as I continue to be a sex and dating writer and stand-up comedian in my adulthood (huge Red Flag).

I personally want to apologize to my favorite ex, Erik, for saying anything bad about the *Fast & Furious* franchise. It was a joke, and those movies rock. Thanks (I'm not kidding) for making me watch all thirteen of them.

I want to thank every guy I've ever dated, flirted with, matched with, or didn't match with on an app; spoken to at a bar or in class or at an event or ever; or did any of these things to my friends, girl, or person. Actually, I just want to thank every guy who was ever born for being a never-ending source of inspiration. Be better! Or don't . . . if the sex is really good.

Lastly, thank you to my future husband for loving me unconditionally despite all my Red Flags, for being a partner, a friend, and unbelievably well-adjusted—but also sexy. I know you're out there, and I'm excited to meet you.

FIRST PUBLISHED IN THE UNITED STATES IN 2026
BY RIZZOLI UNIVERSE, A DIVISION OF
RIZZOLI INTERNATIONAL PUBLICATIONS, INC.
49 WEST 27TH STREET · NEW YORK, NY 10001
RIZZOLIUSA.COM

PUBLISHER: CHARLES MIERS
ASSOCIATE PUBLISHER: JESSICA FULLER
EDITOR: SARAH M. SUTHERLAND
PRODUCTION MANAGER: COLIN HOUGH-TRAPP

DESIGNED BY CMYKAYLEIGH

TYPESET IN BELY, GARALDA, AND MR EAVES

PRINTED IN CHINA

2026 2027 2028 2029 / 10 9 8 7 6 5 4 3 2 1
ISBN: 978-0-7893-4620-9
LIBRARY OF CONGRESS CONTROL NUMBER: 2025940209

THE AUTHORIZED REPRESENTATIVE IN THE EU FOR PRODUCT SAFETY AND COMPLIANCE IS MONDADORI LIBRI S.P.A.
VIA GIAN BATTISTA VICO 42 · MILAN, ITALY, 20123
MONDADORI.IT

VISIT US ONLINE:
INSTAGRAM.COM/RIZZOLIBOOKS
FACEBOOK.COM/RIZZOLINEWYORK
YOUTUBE.COM/USER/RIZZOLINY